found
faithful

*f*ound
*f*aithful

WILLIAM GILMORE

AMBASSADOR

Found Faithful
First published 1940

This edition published by
Ambassador Productions Ltd
Providence House
16 Hillview Avenue
Belfast, BT5 6JR

ISBN 1 898787 03 4

CONTENTS.

PUBLISHER'S PREFACE TO THIS EDITION

In these studies, William Gilmore seeks to retain the essential simplicity of the characters he has chosen to profile. Allowing them to live and move and touch our lives with a vibrant immediacy and unmistakable clarity.

Although written over fifty years ago, a new generation of Christians will profit from this book.

FOREWORD.

THOUGH this book, I am convinced, needs no commendation from me, I should be thankful if I could say anything to further its usefulness. It is composed in large part, if not in whole, of addresses which the author has delivered before companies of the Lord's people, and we feel sure that those who have listened to our brother's platform ministry will be glad to have it before them in this more permanent form. I heartily commend it to the Lord's people, young or old. The papers of which it is composed present in a very fresh and full way certain Bible characters, including Gideon, some of David's honourables and mighty men, Elijah, Daniel, and two papers on Paul as the model Christian, from Philippians 3 and 2 Timothy 3.

One feels in reading these studies that they are the fruit of much meditation on the Word; they are lessons learned in "the Secret Place," and one is thankful to notice that the writer avoids two evils: on the one hand the unhealthy tendency, which displays itself to-day too commonly, of continually judging the Lord's servants of Bible fame, exaggerating weaknesses or failures, regarding which the Scriptures are silent. It is scarcely for this object that God has left us the record of His saints' warfare. On the other hand he avoids glorying in man and putting these heroes of God on an inaccessible pedestal. It is not man that is magnified, but the grace of God in them, and the reader is humbled in the presence of God and made to feel that that same grace is for him for the service to which God has called him, and which through sloth or sin or unbelief he may miss.

W. HOSTE.

The Model Christian.

(Phil. 3.).

PAUL was the model Christian, and his life as recorded in this chapter is worthy of special study. Throughout the whole passage he presents his own experience as the type to which ours ought to be conformed. We have

I.

PAUL STRIPPING.

"Those I counted loss for Christ" (v. 7).

HE begins by recounting his privileges, noting each item with great distinctness. If any had ground for confidence in the flesh, he had more. He was circumcised the eighth day. This right which introduced him to the covenant of Abraham had been performed exactly when ordained by the law, and not as proselytes were in later life. He was of the

9

stock of Israel—descended by a clear line from that Israel who was a prince with God. He was of the tribe of Benjamin—the tribe which Moses called "the beloved of the Lord," and the tribe from which the first king of Israel had been chosen. He was a Hebrew of the Hebrews—that is of Hebrew lineage on both sides. As touching the law he was a Pharisee. He belonged to that sect which attached importance to the very minutest details of the law. As to personal character he was full of zeal, persecuting the Church. This he had done in all honesty of heart as the result of his own self-righteousness. Finally, as touching the righteousness which was in the law he was blameless. "All these grounds for self-satisfaction were like triple armour round the heart of the young Pharisee." But suddenly that armour was pierced and his proud heart reached and conquered. Now what was it which wrought so sudden and so deep a change in this man? It was the heavenly vision seen on the way to Damascus —the revelation of Christ in glory. In the light of that wonderful revelation he poured contempt upon all his natural and religious advantages. Instead of glorying in them he thought of them as only refuse, something to be got rid of. He said, "What things were gain to me those I counted loss for Christ."

To gain Him he stripped himself of all the things in which he formerly boasted. The discernment of Christ as the one ground of his confidence was at once followed by the casting away of every other. His own right-eousness which was of the law he had done with for ever—he had found something better.

II.

PAUL CLOTHING.

"And be found in Him" (v. 9).

PAUL never regretted his early choice. After long years of Christian experience he still stands to the estimate made at con-version, 'Yea doubtless: and I count all things but loss for the excellency of the knowledge of Christ Jesus my Lord: for whom I have suffered the loss of all things and do count them but dung that I may gain Christ." He had suffered the loss of all things in more senses than one. He had no worldly property. He had no provision for future needs. But he had Christ, and to him Christ was all. He speaks of Him as "my Lord." Surely no sweeter language could be used by mortal lips. When Christ is enthroned in the heart there is no difficulty in giving up all things for Him. He becomes at once the object of our love, the source of our satisfaction, the theme of our praise and our all in all. It is an inspiring sight to see this model saint standing just where he stood at first—at the beginning of his Christian course. He was perfectly satisfied to "be found in Him," satisfied to be in Him for safety and shelter as fugitives take refuge in a strong tower when pressed by the foe. Samuel Rutherford uses this expression—"I wrap me up in Christ." That is what Paul did and that is what we have all done if we are really saved. But I believe the expression "be found in Him" reaches beyond the limits of time. It contains a clear reference to that day that is coming. We think of other instances of the use of that same expression which point to that day, for example, "Being clothed we shall not be found naked," or, "Be found of Him in peace without spot and blameless." We have in Christ a righteousness which cannot fail us either in time or in eternity..

"E'en treading the valley, the shadow of death,
  This watchword shall rally my faltering breath;
  And when from life's fever my God sets me free,
  Jehovah-Tsidkenu my death song shall be."

III.

PAUL STUDYING.

"That I may know Him" (v. 10).

"THAT I may know Him, and the power of His resurrection, and the fellowship of His sufferings, being made conformable unto His death, if by any means I might attain unto the resurrection from among the dead." This was Paul's aim in life, and it was passionately pursued. He already knew something of Christ but was longing to know more. It was no mere intellectual knowledge which he aimed at but personal acquaintance with Christ. This knowledge cannot be acquired in schools nor gleaned from books. In this way we may get to know many things about Him, but to know Himself we need to live in communion with Him. To deepen our knowledge of Christ in this way is a worthy aim for the whole of life. Some knowledge puffs up but this knowledge will make us humble. Most of the subjects which we study down here will be forgotten in the world to come, but the knowledge of Christ will abide with us for ever. It will still be

13

pursued amid eternal glories. Christ Himself will be our lesson for eternity.

The Apostle also desired to know the power of His resurrection. This expression refers to the power that flows from the resurrection of Christ. There are several distinct powers ascribed to it in the New Testament. It is spoken of as an evidencing power in reference to our Lord's person and work, for He is by it declared to be the Son of God with power. His resurrection has also a justifying power—"He was raised again for our justification." Christ's resurrection has also a comforting power as to all departed saints. As surely as He rose, all those who are His shall rise also. When the trumpet blast shall wake the dead the graves shall give up their spoils. This assurance comes to us through Jesus' empty tomb, "Hallelujah, Christ arose." But His resurrection has a quickening power even now. It calls upon us to seek the things that are above where Christ sitteth at the right hand of God. In Him we are raised to walk in newness of life. In this experimental sense we all need to know more of the power of His resurrection. But experience of the power of His resurrection is inseparable from "the fellowship of His sufferings." To suffer for Christ is to suffer with Him, and in His fellowship we shall find strength to endure

14

and patience to outlast any sufferings that may come to us because we belong to Him.

Paul's hope of a place in the first resurrection encouraged him to bear whatever sufferings crossed his pathway. "If by any means I might attain unto the resurrection from among the dead." The hypothetical form of these words does not imply a doubt as to the final issue but speaks of the earnestness of the struggle. With the certainty of resurrection glory before him he did not mind what suffering lay between. He looked forward with joyful anticipation to the last result of the power of Christ's resurrection—the perfect transformation of spirit, soul and body into the perfect likeness of his Lord.

IV.

PAUL RUNNING.

"I press toward the mark" (v. 14).

PAUL had been "apprehended of Christ Jesus"—that's how he describes what we call his conversion. Christ gripped him and drew him to Himself for a special purpose. It was Paul's life aim to know and attain to all that Christ has saved him for, but to this he had not attained. He says, "Not as though I had already attained either were already perfect; but I follow after, if that I may apprehend that for which I am apprehended of Christ Jesus." This is the language of one who was vastly superior to any of us in Christian life and experience. Where can we find a man so fully consecrated as Paul was? Yet he says, "I have not attained, I am not yet perfect."

This letter to the Philippians was written many years after that day on the road to Damascus, yet with all these years of experience and progress behind him he says, "I follow after." It was the one passion of his soul to press on toward the great goal of his hopes. With this in view he had no time to cast his eye over his shoulder to mark the steps already trod. He says, "Forgetting the things that are behind, and reaching forth unto those things which are before, I press toward the mark for the prize of the high calling of God in Christ Jesus."

The Apostle uses a very graphic word here translated "reaching forth." It contains a picture of the runner with his whole body thrown forward and his hand extended in eager anticipation of the prize. It implies the putting forth of every exertion and the straining of every nerve to obtain that which he desired. "This one thing I do." Oh that we all had more of Paul's burning earnestness and whole-hearted concentration on the life that pleases God. It was his earnest desire that others should think and do according to the pattern set forth in this chapter, "Let as many as be perfect be thus minded." These perfect people were not sinless people. When the Epistle to the Hebrews speaks of them that are of full age, the same word is used as in this passage. It means full grown, as in contrast with babes, and does not express absolute completeness. These same perfect people are exhorted to be constantly reaching forth to unattained heights. But it was possible for them to be otherwise minded— that is, otherwise than the rule of life set forth in this chapter. But the Apostle expresses confidence that God will show them any divergence from His pattern for them and bring them into conformity with His will. If the main direction of our life is right—if we really desire to do His will—God will reveal to us the things in which we are wrong. By His Word and His Spirit He will lead us in the old paths and the good way.

The exact phrase, "if in anything ye be otherwise minded," that is not in principle but perhaps in degree.

V.

PAUL WEEPING.

"And now tell you even weeping" (v. 18).

PAUL was no soft piece of sentiment and seldom shed a tear even under grievous trials. Do we ever read of him weeping when he was persecuted? When he was cast into prison, we read of his singing but never of his sighing. Then why does this courageous man weep now? Ah, he was thinking of some professed followers of Christ who had gone far astray, and of whom he had warned the Philippians often. As he thought of their unholy conduct and their awful doom, it drew the tears from his eyes even in the midst of his joys. Who these unworthy professors were is somewhat obscure. They are characterized as enemies of the Cross of Christ. They seem to have shaken off the restraints of common morality and were living for self-indulgence. They were also out and out worldlings—they minded earthly things. Little wonder the Apostle wept as he thought of them. If we had more of his tender-heartedness we might weep too. There are still many

18

who bear the name of Christ who by their ways show that there is not a breath of divine life in them. Professing to know God in works they deny Him. In these last days profession is made easy, and it is not difficult to be formally in fellowship with the people of God. But let us not be deceived. If the main current of a life is in the direction of worldliness and sin, there can be only one end to that life, and that is destruction.

But from this dark picture the Apostle now turns to the bright hope of the true Christian.

VI.

PAUL WATCHING.

"We look for the Saviour" (v. 20).

"FOR our conversation is in heaven: from whence also we look for the Saviour, the Lord Jesus Christ: who shall change our vile body that it may be fashioned like unto His glorious body, according to the working whereby He is able even to subdue all things unto Himself." These stirring words lift our thoughts and affections above. They tell us of our heavenly home and our heavenly hope. That heavenly home is ours because He is there for whom we wait and watch. The eagerness of the watching is beautifully described by the Apostle's expression for it. "The word means to look away out: like a sentry on the walls of a besieged city whose eyes are fixed on the pass amongst the hills through which the relieving forces are to come." In this expectant way we are to look for the coming Saviour. He has promised to come and will surely keep His tryst with His people. Our path may be beset with trials and difficulties now, but He is coming to save us out of them all. Our salvation will be complete when He comes. He is coming to raise the sleeping saints, and to charge all those who are alive and remain unto His coming. This was Paul's hope and it is ours. The bodies of our humiliation are now made up of decaying substances, but at His coming they will be made like unto the body of His glory. We cannot explain the process by which we shall be transfigured into His likeness but we know by what power it will be accomplished, according to the working whereby He is able even to subdue all things unto Himself. With such a blessed hope in view Paul exhorts the Philippians and us to stedfastness in the faith—"Stand fast in the Lord my dearly beloved." This is the watchword for the people of God in these days.

FOUND FAITHFUL.

Many are drifting with the tide and driven by every wind, but let us hearken to no teaching but that which comes from Holy Scripture. We must not budge an inch from the old doctrines and the old paths. May we all be found faithful to Him and to His Word when He appears. At the battle of Waterloo a hard-pressed officer sent a message to the Commander-in-Chief asking permission to remove from his position. The reply he received was —"Every Englishman to-day must die where he stands or win the victory." And he did stand until the victory was won. "So stand fast in the Lord my dearly beloved." It will only be a little while until the trumpet shall sound for our everlasting victory.

> "This day the noise of battle,
> The next the victor's song."

Paul's Letter to Timothy.

I TRUST we all read very often Paul's second
epistle to Timothy. Three things make it
specially and deeply interesting to us.

1. It was his last letter, written from the
banks of the river just before he crossed to
the better land. So it ought to come to us as
a voice from eternity. We should hear it with
the same interest and earnestness with which
we listen to the last words of our dearest
friends. Here we have the very last words of
the great Apostle to the Gentiles, whose life
and letters have been an inspiration to count-
less thousands of God's people. Every word
has a weight which demands our special attention in these last days.

2. It was written to Timothy, his beloved
son, so he opens up his heart in a way he
does not do anywhere else. He had known
Timothy from the beginning of his second
missionary journey, and their hearts were
closely knit together in the bonds of Christian
love and gospel fellowship. Timothy seems
to have been weak in body and troubled with
"often infirmities." He was probably timid

and sensitive—easily depressed in face of difficulties. He was certainly of softer material than the old warrior who was just going off the field. Timothy now stood at the darkest hour of his whole life. His trusted leader and counsellor was soon to be removed. He was soon to be left lonely and exposed in face of a world of thronging sorrows and difficulties. Little wonder if he needed bracing up. For this purpose Paul's letter was written to him. It is full of parting counsels which sound like trumpet blasts to stir up his courage for the conflict. He exhorts him to zeal, courage and stedfastness, and warns him against cowardice, unfaithfulness and worldliness. He wants him to endure hardness as a good soldier of Jesus Christ. Present ease and comfort formed no part of Paul's programme for the servant of God. He wanted a man who could face the foe and lift high the banner of the cross when the old standard-bearer had joined the ranks above.

3. It describes for us the characteristics of the last days. It leads us to expect, among other things, a great apostacy from the truth. It has more to say of troublesome individuals than any of Paul's writings. They are mostly named in couples. Phygellus and Hermogenes, Hymenæus and Philetus, Jannes and Jambres, Demas and Alexander—these last two are

named separately. These individuals seem to be chief examples of the apostacy of that time, and their names mark different stages in its progress. In Phygellus and Hermogenes we have "Defection" or turning away from the truth. In Hymenæus and Philetus we have "Counteraction" or opposing the truth by teaching positive error. These false teachers were the advanced thinkers of that time. Their successors are still with us. In Jannes and Jambres we have "Imitation." As these magicians withstood Moses by imitating his miracles as far as they could, so these evil workers of Paul's day resisted the truth by imitating it. This was a very subtle form of opposition to the truth, and many were deceived by it, and many are deceived by it still. The successors of Jannes and Jambres find imitation easier than it was in the days of Moses. It is now no question of miracle but only the semblance of truth. They can profess the same opinions and use the same phraseology as true Christians. They can speak highly of the Scriptures while at the same time trying to undermine them. Their teaching on sin and salvation is not the Bible doctrine of these subjects. Their "future retribution" is not eternal punishment as taught in the Scriptures. Their gospel is one out of which the gospel has been drained, and which wouldn't save a fly.

In Demas we have "Desertion." "Demas hath forsaken me, having loved this present age." He was a Christian but a coward. He deserted Paul at a time when his help was most needed. He preferred the friendship of the world and so saved his own skin. He went to Thessalonica just to be out of the way of the dungeon.

In Alexander we have "Persecution." He may have been a professed disciple, but he was a real enemy of Paul and of the Gospel, for he withstood the words of the preachers. He was evidently a wolf in sheep's clothing, hence Timothy was to be on guard against him.

Now how did this condition of things affect Paul's spirit? There he was an old man, a prisoner, poor and thinly clad, forsaken by his friends, hated by his foes, despised by the learned, ridiculed by the ignorant. Was he disheartened? Well, he was only human and must have felt these things as keenly as any of us would do. But he was divinely sustained, so he rose triumphant over all the seeming wreck and said, "I suffer these things yet I am not ashamed, I am not disappointed." There is not a despondent note in this dying letter. It is full of the ministry of good cheer. What sustained him? What were the secrets of his joyful confidence? He had

I.

AN ALMIGHTY SAVIOUR
(Chap. 1. 12).

1. "I KNOW whom I have believed and am persuaded that He is able to keep that which I have committed unto Him against that day." He did not say, "I know what I have believed." Surely he did know that every Christian ought to know what he believes and why he believes it. In these days we have some professing Christians who seem to believe anything and a few who believe nothing. But Paul was not satisfied with mere doctrine, for that alone cannot satisfy the heart. Truth must never be separated from the Person of Christ. In Him all truth has life and power. Can we all say, "I know Him." No other knowledge is of such real value both for time and for eternity. Then let us go in for more of it. But how did Paul know Him? He knew Him by blessed experience. Ever since that memorable day, when he was suddenly transformed from a bitter persecutor to a devout worshipper, he knew Him. He knew Him as the Bearer of his sins. He knew Him as the satisfying

27

object of his heart. He knew Him as the Friend that sticketh closer than a brother. He knew Him as his Lord and Master. He knew Him as the life-long subject of his study. He gave up all that he might know Him and the power of His resurrection and the fellowship of His sufferings. He knew Him as perhaps no other saint ever did know Him. He was filled and thrilled through his whole being with the excellency of the knowledge of Christ Jesus his Lord.

2. He committed to His keeping all his temporal and eternal interests. He committed to Him his soul for safe keeping throughout time and eternity. He also committed to Him his body. It was soon to be the prey of Nero's cruelty, but he committed it to Him who is the resurrection and the life. He gave into His keeping his character and reputation. He had been misunderstood, misrepresented and misused, but for honour he could wait until that day when the counsels of the heart shall be made manifest and every man shall have praise of God. Into His hands he delivered his life-work, and what a wonderful work it was. We are reaping the benefit of it to this day. His service met with poor reward down here, but it shall have a full reward in the crowning day that's coming. There is no risk to anything we commit to the keeping of

Christ. In His hands our interests are all safe and always safe. He is able to keep that which we commit to Him against that day. Of this Paul was fully assured. His strong confidence was founded on knowledge. "I know whom I have believed." There was no doubt as to whether he had believed or not, he knew he had believed. There was no question as to whether he was quite safe in believing, he says, "I am persuaded." That implies that he had thought the matter over, had meditated upon it, and the power of truth had fully persuaded him. He speaks as one who cannot tolerate a doubt. He has absolutely no fear for the future. He is as positive for the time to come as for the time then present. He knew his deposit was safe until that day. But what day was he thinking of? There was no need to say what day. There were only two days in Paul's calendar. This day of toil and that day of rest. This day of service and that day of reward. This day of suffering and that day of glory. This day of expectation and that day of realization. How it must have heartened up young Timothy to find the dying saint so full of faith and courage. May it cheer us all up, for Paul's Almighty Saviour is our Saviour too.

II.

THE IMMOVABLE FOUNDATION
(Chap. 2. 19).

NOW look for a few minutes at another great truth which gave Paul comfort and courage in his difficulties. He had just been speaking of Hymenæus and Philetus who had overthrown the faith of some, but he found his refuge in that which is indestructible: the foundation of God standeth sure. Whatever may happen, whoever may go away, however unfaithful men may be, God's foundation remains immovable. But what is the foundation here referred to? In this passage the metaphor seems to stand for whatever is founded by God: that remains secure whatever else may happen. Ungodliness may increase, the love of many may wax cold, errors may threaten to flood the Church, some may turn away of whom better was expected. "Nevertheless the foundation of God standeth sure." Oh, it is a joy to quit the moving flood for the rock which cannot be shaken. A number of men were engaged in lifting a shaft into position in a mill, but although they seemed to put their whole strength to the work, they were unable to lift it. Then the foreman noticed that the scaffold was not quite secure —it yielded just a little under the extra pressure; so the men were not really using their full strength because they did not feel quite safe themselves. If we are not sure of our own standing and security we can never be strong in the service of God. But if we are really on God's foundation we are safe for time and for eternity.

The purpose of God remains immovable. Though men may prove unfaithful still His purpose must be carried out. He has a purpose both in creation and redemption from which He can never swerve. His purpose shall stand and He will do all His pleasure.

The Word of God remains immovable. Paul had been speaking of the great fundamental truth of resurrection which the false teachers said was past already, but it was not past for all that. The opinions of men can never change the truth of God. They have disproved the doctrine of atonement by blood, but the doctrine is still true. They have denied the Deity of Christ, but still He is God over all blessed for ever. No truth of God can ever be destroyed by the fires through which it may pass.

31

The work of God remains immovable. His work in the salvation of His people cannot be overthrown. His work in the preservation of His Church cannot be overthrown. The House of God still stands and the gates of hell shall not prevail against it. The foundation of God has a seal which gives the divine guarantee for our security. "The Lord knoweth them that are His." Some who take His name are not really His and He knows them not. But if we have really trusted Christ we are His by election, by redemption, by conversion, by sanctification. We are His for ever. When God knows us as His He will preserve us and keep us to the end. It is a blessed thing to be sure that God knows us when the world does not know us. When we are so tumbled up and down in our minds that we hardly know ourselves, still He knows us. When our brethren don't know us, and perhaps don't want to know us, the Lord knows us just the same. Some preacher gave an interesting address on the question, "Shall we know one another in heaven?" Soon after a member of his congregation wrote suggesting that he might preach some day on the question, "Is it possible to know one another here?" and he added, "I have been attending your church for six months now and no one has spoken to me yet." Now that's a very practical way of putting it. If we believe that we shall know one another in heaven, let us strike up a closer acquaintance before we get there. The practical should always go with the doctrinal. That reminds us of the other inscription on the seal, "Let every one that nameth the name of the Lord depart from iniquity." To name the name of the Lord is to say that we are His and the best proof that we really belong to Him is our living the life of practical righteousness and holiness. Every true Christian should depart from iniquity as the Israelites departed from Egypt.

Let us not dishonour that holy name wherewith we are named. Let us seek after the greatest measure of practical godliness. We need to think far more than we do of our influence upon others. We are either lights or stumbling-blocks in this dark world of sin. Much present-day Christianity consists chiefly in running to meetings and singing hymns. But it is quite possible to do that and have no vital godliness behind it. It is awfully possible to revel in doctrine and live in sin. May it be ours to have truth in the inward parts and holiness to the Lord to the core of our hearts.

III.

THE INFALLIBLE BOOK
(Chap. 3. 16).

NOW we come to the great passage about inspiration. Paul had not only an Almighty Saviour and an immovable foundation, he had also an infallible Book. He says, "All Scripture is given by inspiration of God, that is, it is God-breathed. The process of inspiration may be beyond our knowledge, but the result is patent. The Bible has proved itself both infallible and indestructible. The divine inspiration of Scripture extends to every part of it—every book from Genesis to Revelation—its histories, prophecies, types, narratives, miracles, parables, are all inspired of God. It includes the record of the sinful words and deeds of men and of Satan. The Holy Spirit has faithfully recorded all such things for our instruction and warning—the record of them is therefore part of the Word of God. It extends to the form as well as the substance, the words as well as the thoughts, "Not in the words which man's wisdom teacheth, but which the Holy Ghost teacheth." To use the language of Gregory the great—the

34

Bible is "the heart of God in the words of God." We have the very same evils to contend with to-day as Paul had in his day, but thank God we have also the same remedy. Continuance in the Word of God will hold us fast against all the seductions of the age. To this unerring guide young Timothy was committed both for salvation and service. From childhood he had known the Holy Scriptures, and he was to continue in the things which he had learnt and of which he had been made sure. He was to stay in them, to find his home there, and to be always at home. Timothy was "a man of God," and it is one of the marks of a man of God that he is at home in the Book of God. In the Old Testament "the man of God" was the popular name for a prophet, one who told out God's message, one who spoke the words that God gave him to speak. Now if we are to be faithful witnesses for God we must get our message from the Scriptures of Truth, "Preach the Word." I think that's why we find the expression "man of God" in connection with the declaration, "All Scripture is given by inspiration of God." By the Scriptures the man of God is to be completely furnished or fitted out for the work to which he has been called. Having the Scriptures hidden in his heart he is prepared to meet all the dangers of these last days. The Scriptures contain all we need to know for life and godliness. This passage names four ways in which the Scriptures are profitable. (1) For teaching or doctrine. The Epistle to the Hebrews is a striking example of this, it sets forth the great truths of the Gospel from the very words and figures of the Old Testament. (2) For reproof or correction. The Epistle to the Galatians is an instance of this. Certain portions of the Old Testament are used to convict the Judaizers of their mistakes. (3) For correction, the tenth chapter of 1 Corinthians may be taken as an example of this use of Scripture. (4 For instruction in righteousness. The Epistle to the Romans is perhaps one of the best specimens of Scripture in this particular way. But if we are to feel and know the practical power of the Bible in our own experience, we must read it and get to know it. We need to read it carefully because it is God's message to us, and every word is of infinite value. We need to read it prayerfully because we need the help of the Holy Spirit in understanding it. We need to read it daily because it is the food of the soul and the soul needs daily bread as well as the body. We need to read it all. There is nothing in it God does not want us to know. He wants us to know all that is revealed of His mind and will for us. May one result of this message be that we shall all have an increased desire for the precious Word of God.

Now we come to the last point, Paul had,

IV.

AN UNFAILING HOPE
(Chap. 4.).

HE says, "The Lord shall deliver me from every evil work, and will preserve me unto His heavenly kingdom to whom be glory for ever and ever. Amen."

Apart from the few personal salutations these are the very last words of this greatest of saints. So his life closes with an utterance of unfaltering faith and a note of heart-felt praise. Surely a fitting close to a devoted life. He had long before expressed the desire to depart and be with Christ which is far better, now the desire is about to be gratified, the time of his departure is at hand. The word rendered departure in verse 6 means a setting free, the untying of a cord, the weighing of an anchor to set the voyager free for that other shore. But before he waved his farewell

37

1. He looked backward over his life and said, "I have fought a good fight, I have finished my course, I have kept the faith." These words describe his life as a contest, a race, and a stewardship. In the contest he had the same foes to contend with that every Christian has against him to this day—the world, the flesh, and the Devil. But in the strength of the Lord he fought and conquered. In the race he had completed the course marked out for him by the Lord. To finish the course means more than to end it. It had been the aspiration of Paul's life "that I might finish my course." Now that aspiration is realized. He had run according to the heavenly programme so he could truthfully say, "I have finished my course." In the stewardship he had been found faithful. He had many temptations to give up the faith, the body of truth believed, but he kept it faithfully to the end. This was a blessed test of faithfulness to his Lord and Master.

2. He looked forward and said, "Henceforth there is laid up for me a crown which the Lord the righteous judge shall give me at that day and not to me only, but to all them also that love His appearing." Through grace he had lived out the fact that he was fully the Lord's, so he looked forward to his rest

and his crown. A man is not crowned except he strive lawfully. But he was to receive the victor's crown from the hand of the righteous judge of the contest, the race and the stewardship.

3. He looked around. His heart longed for the fellowship of some whom he missed. Only Luke remained with him, faithful unto death. His attitude to the Lord's devoted servant was a true index of his attitude to the Master Himself. His heart was cheered at the remembrance of a time when all forsook him, but the Lord stood with him and strengthened him. With Christ at his side nothing could shake his stedfast heart. So now he looked forward to his final deliverance. The Lord shall deliver me from every evil work. But wasn't he martyred. Yes, but the martyrdom was the deliverance. One stroke of the gleaming sword and Paul's ransomed spirit was at home in the presence of the One he had loved so long and served so well. May we have grace to follow him as he followed Christ. To this end let us take a firmer grip of the great hold-fasts of the faith—the Almighty Saviour, the immovable foundation, the infallible Book and the unfailing hope, and they will hold us fast through all the storms of life until that day.

39

Devotedness to Christ

(2 Sam. 15. and 23).

I WANT to speak a little on Devotedness to
Christ. The passages we have read give us
some striking illustrations of that subject. We
have here a list of David's honourables—
those who did valiantly for him in the time
of his rejection. Their valour was manifested
in different ways and in different degrees, but
the mainspring of all was their love for David.
They loved him both for his personal worth
and for his great work. He had proved himself fit to be their leader and commander, so
they were all passionately devoted to him.
They were David's men, his for life and his
for death. They all believed in the ultimate
triumph of his cause. They knew he was
God's anointed and that he would certainly
reach the throne, so they were all of one heart
to see him crowned king. 2 Samuel 23. shows
that when David was king he did not forget
those who had done valiantly for him in the
days of his rejection. So David's Son and

41

David's Lord will recount His worthies by-and-by, and everything done for His glory shall have a full reward. May we all be stirred up to love Him more and serve Him better in this day of opportunity.

I.

ITTAI: THE MAN WHO WOULDN'T BE DISCOURAGED.

BEFORE we speak of chapter 23, look for a moment at the case of Ittai as illustrating one aspect of devotedness to Christ. David did not encourage this man to risk his life for his sake seeing he had only come over to his side a short time ago, but Ittai wouldn't be discouraged. His answer shows that he was all for David whether in life or death. He said, "Surely in what place my Lord the King shall be, whether in death or life, even there also will thy servant be."

1. This is the language of pure love. He dedicated himself to David when he was newly come to him—a young convert. Oh, what wonders God might work in you and through you if you were fully dedicated to

Christ and His cause in the palmy days of your youth. Ittai's example should be an inspiration to us all. If he could be so out and out for David, how much more should we dedicate ourselves to the heavenly David and say, "Surely in whatever place my Lord and Saviour shall be, whether in death or life, even there also will thy servant be." It was Ittai's pure love for David that kept him from being discouraged. There are not too many of his kind in the Church of God in these times. Most of us are far too easily discouraged. But if our hearts are really true to the Lord, He will give us grace to go on for Him even in discouraging circumstances.

2. Ittai's speech is—The language of self-sacrifice. His vow was made when David's fortunes were at the very lowest ebb. It meant, "I'm ready to suffer, to lose everything, to die if need be in order to be true to thee." He cast in his lot with David for better or worse, and he meant to be with him to the end. He was filled with a passionate attachment to him and that attachment was ready to manifest itself in willing sacrifice as true love always does. The joy of unselfish love is the purest joy that a man can taste. Ittai was no secret follower of David; he took sides with him publicly, when he was sur-

rounded by rebels. He marched in front where all could see him. Henceforth he was to be David's servant and he was not ashamed of his service. Oh, if we all loved Christ as this man loved David, we would give ourselves, all we are and have, more fully to Him, in this day of His rejection. The more His claims are set at nought by the world the stronger should be our loyalty to Him.

3. Ittai's speech is the language of restful delight in the presence of the one whom his heart loved. He just wanted to be with David wherever he was. Love always seeks to get near to its object. So we should seek to be in the company and fellowship of our David, as near to Him as we can possibly be. But how can we get nearer to Him? Where can we find Him? We may always find Him in the Scriptures. He says, "They are they which testify of Me." Through the written Word we may get into contact with the Living Word. Then let us never be far away from a Bible. Again, we may always find Him with His gathered people. He always keeps His promise, "Where two or three are gathered together in My name, there am I in the midst of them." If there is a place on earth where He manifests Himself to His people it is where the bread is broken in remembrance of

Him. Then let us seek to gather around Himself according to His Word unless prevented by things over which we have no control. Again, we shall find Him in heaven when we get there. To see Him as He is and to be with Him for ever will be the consummation of all our joys. "I shall be satisfied when I awake with His likeness."

II.

ELEAZAR: THE MAN WHO WOULDN'T LET GO.

NOW turn to chapter 23. In verses 9-10 we read of the heroism of Eleazar. We learn three things concerning him.

1. He was in a conflict. In this he is a picture of every true Christian. To be a Christian is to be a warrior. This world is not a flowery bed of ease: it is a real battlefield. The way to heaven is beset with spiritual foes. To be in conflict with these powers of darkness is no sham battle. The forces of evil are at war against Christ and His cause as surely as the Philistines were against David and his cause. If we are really on the Lord's side, we

must be in the fight against these powers of evil. It is not enough that we are not conquered by them: we must seek to conquer. We must carry the warfare into the enemy's territory. In other words we must be aggressive in the cause of God in these perilous times. We need to combat error by spreading the truth. Eleazar fought the Philistines, and the Lord wrought a great victory through him. God loves to see His people victorious. He has no pleasure in their defeat.

2. Eleazar had a sword, without it he could not have won the battle. So the Lord has provided His warriors with a sword for the spiritual conflict, and what a wonderful sword it is. You remember how Bunyan describes it: "Then said Mr. Greatheart to Mr. Valiant-for truth, Thou hast worthily behaved thyself; let me see thy sword. So he showed it him. When he had taken it into his hand and looked thereon awhile, he said, Ha, it is a right Jerusalem blade: Then said Mr. Valiant-for-truth, It is so. Let a man have one of these blades, with a hand to wield it, and skill to use it, and he may venture upon an angel with it. He need not fear its holding if he can but tell how to lay on. Its edge will never blunt. It will cut flesh and bones and soul and spirit and all." That's a good description of the

sword of the Spirit which is the Word of God. It is the only weapon of offence provided for the spiritual warfare, and it is sufficient.

But, as Bunyan says, we need skill to use it. Eleazar, the man who wouldn't let go, will give us a lesson on this. He had skill to use his sword. He held it with so firm a grip that his hand clave to it. So if we would fight the Lord's battles we must not hold His truth with a slack hand.

In these days of letting go we need to tighten our grip and earnestly contend for the faith once delivered to the saints. "That which ye have already hold fast till I come." Eleazar had full confidence in his sword. His hand was weary but he held on. He was not thinking of his own comforts but only of fighting David's battles. We may also learn something from Paul on this matter of using the sword. He was a very skilful swordsman and used it as one who believed it to be quick and powerful. Let me remind you of one occasion when he used it with effect. When he healed the cripple at Lystra the people said, "The gods are come down to us in the likeness of men." No doubt the great adversary of his soul was behind that attempt to elate him and inflate him, but immediately he drew the sword and defeated his foe with a word from the 146th Psalm.

But to learn best how to use this sword we need to be much in company with the Lord Himself. He never drew it in vain. When the tempter put before Him his threefold temptation, immediately He used the sword. His master stroke was "It is written." Most of us could probably recall times in our own experience when we have had to use the same sword to slay our doubts and fears and temptations.

I remember my first visit to Glasgow as a youth of nineteen. Bradlaugh, the noted infidel, was lecturing there at the time. Youthful curiosity mastered me so far that I went to the Waterloo Rooms to hear what he had to say. As I entered the hall a text of Scripture came to my remembrance with great power, "Cease my son to hear the instruction that causeth to err from the words of knowledge." So when the sword of the Spirit blocked the way I thought it safer to turn back, and I never heard Bradlaugh, for which I am thankful.

III.

SHAMMAH: THE MAN WHO WOULDN'T SURRENDER.

1. THIS man stood when others fled. The popular thing would have been to go with the crowd, but Shammah dared to be singular. He might have thought the case hopeless; he might have reasoned, "What can one Israelite do against so many Philistines?" But in the strength of God he made a stand and won a great victory. He is an inspiring sight for discouraged saints. We learn from him what God can do through one whole-hearted man. If only one man will stop running away and stand for God victory is certain. Shammah won the battle with what was left of the defeat. We are constantly being reminded that collective testimony has failed and cannot be restored, so some give up standing for anything and run after everything—they join the Nothingarians. This is not God's way. Do what Shammah did— stand in what's left of the defeat and win. It is never too late to stand for God and His truth. When one man stands firm he becomes a rallying point for others. When one Christian gets a victory it encourages all, at least it

49

should encourage us all, for we ought to be able to rejoice in the success of others.

2. Shammah had a big fight for a seemingly small thing—a plot of lentils. But then they were Israel's lentils, so he wouldn't allow the Philistines to have them. His motto, his battle cry was, "No surrender." But difficulties will meet us even in standing our ground. The Philistines will rob us of the things most surely believed among us if they can. Victory must be won by fighting. We should never consider any part of God's truth of small importance. Some drop one thing and some another for the sake of a little short-lived popularity. We hear a great deal of the reunion of the churches, but lasting unity among saints must come by way of the Bible, as Spurgeon said.

In these days of great united efforts and the desire to do things on a huge scale, there is a real danger of being ensnared into a conspiracy of silence about certain truths of the Word of God. More than ever we need to stand for a whole Book and liberty to preach it. We are not sent to offer concessions but to be faithful witnesses for the truth. If we are true to God and His truth we can never compromise. The language of deceit fits not a holy tongue. May we have grace to go on in the old paths till He come.

IV.

THE MEN WHO WOULDN'T STOP AT ANYTHING
(vv. 13-17).

NOW look at the three worthies who
brought water from the well of Bethlehem. It was harvest-time, so David was
tired and hot and thirsty. Then he longed
for one more draught of the water that tasted
so cool and sweet to his memory. Doubtless
many things were struggling through his mind
when he gave expression to this gust of desire
from the very depths of his spirit. Doubtless
he wanted the water to quench his thirst, but
there was more than this in that irresistible
longing that swept across him. Perhaps his
feelings were the same as expressed in that
old hymn:

> "As I wandered round the homestead,
>   Many a dear familiar spot
> Brought within my recollection
>   Things I'd seemingly forgot.
> There the orchard-meadow, yonder,
>   Here, the deep, old-fashioned well
> With its old moss-covered bucket
>   Sent a thrill no tongue can tell."

Possibly David's longing had something
even deeper than that in it. He may have been
thinking of some early spiritual experience

51

associated with that same old well. Don't we all sigh sometimes for the water of the well of Bethlehem. In memory we go back to where we started and think of the days of first love and that early devotion to the Saviour. But whatever may have been the feelings that lay behind David's desire, it was quite sufficient for these heroes to know that he longed for a drink from the well of Bethlehem. They said, "He shall have it." But the ranks of the Philistines stood between them and Bethlehem—how were they to get through? How could three men outmanœuvre an army? Love never stops to calculate. It laughs at impossibilities and cries "it shall be done." These were the men who wouldn't stop at anything. They were ready to die to win for David the draught he desired. So they slipped away and broke through the ranks of the Philistines and brought back the sparkling water. Surely this is a sweet sample of what we ought to be—loving not our lives unto death for Christ's sake. Oh that the spirit of God may kindle in our hearts a flame of ardent love for the Person of Christ. Then it will be our delight to know His will and seek grace to do it.

Then there will be no asking "Is it essential?" "Is it necessary?" "Can we not get to heaven without it?" Enough to know that He desires it—commands it; "If ye love Me keep My commandments." The Lord delights in the service constrained by love—willing whole-hearted service. It is said that there are three kinds of givers in the Church—(1) the flint kind—they give when they're struck; (2) the sponge kind—they give when they're squeezed; (3) the honeycomb kind—they give spontaneously. Now note what David did with the water. It was the expression of a love that was stronger than death, so he would not drink it. He poured it out as a libation to God as though the gift were fit only to be made to Him. It reminds us of that beautiful example of Christian devotedness set forth in Philippians 2, "Yea, and if I be offered upon the sacrifice and service of your faith, I joy and rejoice with you all for the same cause also do ye joy and rejoice with me."

May we all be stirred up to give God our best. May we hear again that rousing appeal, "I beseech you therefore, brethren, by the mercies of God that ye present your bodies a living sacrifice, holy, acceptable to God, which is your reasonable service," and may our hearty response be—

"Take my love: my Lord, I pour
At Thy feet its treasure store
Take myself and I will be
Ever, only, all for Thee."

53

V.

BENAIAH: THE MAN WHO WOULDN'T TURN BACK.

NOW just a few words in closing about Benaiah, the man who wouldn't turn back. He has more than one heroic deed to his account, but we have only time to speak of one. "He went down and slew a lion in the midst of a pit in time of snow." The Spirit of God thought that worth recording, and we should think it worth studying. Benaiah did a difficult thing in a difficult place, and in difficult surroundings.

1. He slew a lion. That was a difficult thing. The Bible has a good deal to say about lion killing.

Some who rose to true greatness had a lion to conquer at the very outset of their career. Samson killed a lion and afterwards found honey in the carcase as a fruit from his victory. David slew both the lion and the bear, and afterwards drew encouragement from that victory to face Goliath, and our blessed Lord Himself in the days of His flesh overcame the one who goes about as a roaring

54

lion seeking whom he may devour. That same lion is still on the track of God's people and we are told to resist him steadfast in the faith. Sometimes the lion attacks us in the form of temptation. We all meet with temptation of various kinds in our every day life. But sometimes a temptation fierce and strong springs on you as the lion sprang on Samson. There is the onrush and pounce of carnal desire. What a conflict many a saint passes through as he struggles with and conquers some sin that besets him like a lion in the way. But temptation can be overcome, the beast can be conquered. There is a blessing promised to those who endure. "Blessed is the man that endureth temptation, for when he is tried he shall receive the crown of life which the Lord hath promised to them that love Him." But we cannot live the overcoming life in our own strength and wisdom. We need to rely on the help and power of the Holy Spirit to make us more than conquerors. There is room for real heroism in the every-day Christian life. Doubtless some of you are resolving even now to go in for a more victorious life in the future, but you must do more than resolve or the bottom may drop out of your resolutions before you get home. You must have personal dealings with God and He can make you an overcomer.

2. Benaiah slew the lion in a difficult place, in a pit. No chance of turning back there. Here's a fight from which there is no escape. It knows no armistice and acknowledges no flag of truce. It is conquer or die. But in the strength of God Benaiah conquered, and so may we. Some of you have to live and work for God in difficult places—some pit where there are few to witness or encourage. But the Lord knows all about it, and He says, "My grace is sufficient for thee, and my strength is made perfect in weakness."

Webb Peploe, after spending two hours preparing a sermon on this text, said: "It is not true. I do not find it sufficient in this heavy trouble that has befallen me." As he wiped his eyes he saw over his table an illuminated text card, which his mother had given him, bearing the same words. The "IS" was bold and in bright green, the "MY" and the "THEE" were both in black letters. A deep and sustaining truth was at once realized. After he told this story in a convention a foreigner came up to him and said, "God bless you for dat 'IS.' When I do get back to my home, I will have him put upon de vall, and he shall be such a great 'IS' as shall make all de people stare."

3. Benaiah slew the lion in difficult circum-

stances, in a time of snow. The surroundings were against him. A snowy day is a cold day, and cold makes the lion more fierce. It is difficult to be courageous on a day like that. It is easier to be heroic when the sun shines and the sky is bright and the birds singing, then you feel like saying, "Are there no foes for me to face?" Many have to live and witness for God in difficult surroundings with nothing to help and no one to cheer. Well, cheer up. In such circumstances Benaiah fought and conquered, and God has placed it on record for your encouragement.

> "From strength to strength go on,
>   Wrestle and fight and pray;
> Tread all the powers of darkness down
>   And win the well-fought day."

Daniel Prospered

(Dan. 6. 28).

THE story of Daniel has its message for to-day. He is one on whose character no blot appears; no sin is ever laid to his charge. There is more detail given concerning the personal life of Daniel than of any other prophet. At the time he was brought as a captive to Babylon he was a youth of about sixteen years, and we read that he continued to the first year of King Cyrus—that is throughout the whole seventy years of captivity; through all the troubles, plots and persecutions this one man stood firm like a pillar amid blowing sands. So while the world and the fashion thereof passeth away, he that doeth the will of God abideth for ever.

I wish briefly to bring before you some things which made Daniel to prosper, and they will make us prosper too if we possess them.

I.

DANIEL PROSPERED BECAUSE HE PURPOSED.

MANY a man's life goes to waste for want of a true and fixed purpose. But Daniel's life was all success because he had a purpose firm, and dared to make it known. He could never have been a man greatly beloved if he had not been a youth greatly decided. He needed all his decision and purpose of character when he went to Babylon. Look at some of the temptations he had to face. He was selected for a three years' course of training to fit him for service in the royal palace. Doubtless this was a great honour, but behind the honour there was danger.

1. His name was changed by his heathen master, and a name taken from the idols of Chaldea was given to him. This was done to make him forget both his country and his god, but in this it failed. The Chaldeans might call him Belteshazzar if they pleased, but Daniel stuck to his old Hebrew name, and calls himself "I Daniel." The name means "God is my judge," and that was the truth

60

that ruled his life. So Daniel stuck to the name that had God in it. Then when God sent his angel-messengers to visit him, they addressed him as "O Daniel." Hundreds of years later when our Lord Himself referred to him, He called him Daniel the prophet. So the names of God's faithful servants are safe in His own keeping, no matter how the world may blacken them.

2. He was to be nourished on the best that the royal table could provide. But the fare would include food and wine that had been first offered to heathen Gods, and to partake of it would mean fellowship with idolatry. It would also include food forbidden to a Hebrew in the book of Leviticus. So Daniel's mind was soon made up. He purposed in his heart that he would not defile himself with the portion of the king's meat nor with the wine which he drank. He would not dishonour the Lord nor compromise with his conscience. The luxuries of a palace were of less value to him than that peace of mind which always follows obedience to the will of God. Doubtless many arguments would be used to persuade him to yield. Somebody would be sure to say, "Why, what difference can it make what you eat or what you drink—there is no use in being so strict about little things." But

nothing could change Daniel's mind. He still purposed in his heart that he would not defile himself, and he kept his purpose. It was well he did. If Daniel had done what he was asked to do, he would have been giving up the separated life, he would have melted into a Chaldean and given up being an Israelite. This is the temptation of the present day. Profess to be a Christian but float along the common current of the world. Perhaps there is some one here to-day who is in a position where he is asked to do what he knows to be wrong, but he says, "I shall be discharged if I refuse to do it." Well, think of Daniel and try to be as straight as he was. The God of Daniel still lives, and He knows how to deliver the godly. Remember the promise, "Come out from among them and be ye separate, saith the Lord, and touch not the unclean thing, and I will receive you, and will be a Father unto you, and ye shall be my sons and daughters, saith the Lord Almighty." Daniel's noble stand for the right led three of his friends to join him, and the story of these four youths who witnessed for God in trying conditions will always have a fascinating interest for all who put principle before everything else.

3. Now note how courteously Daniel de-

clared his purpose. He went to the prince and told him his scruples and requested that he might not be obliged to defile himself. So his firmness of character was adorned by gentleness of manner. There are many ways of doing the same thing, and some people always take the ugliest way of doing everything. They seem to think that rudeness is heroism. But a true Christian should be a true gentleman. Daniel's gentle manner won all hearts and he became a favourite in the Chaldean court. Daniel was willing to have his principles put to the test, and that's why he requested that he and his companions should be fed on pulse and water, and if at the end of their appointed time of testing they were not the better for their plain vegetarian fare they were willing to consider further. But at the end of their trial they were fairer and fatter than all the children which did eat the portion of the king's meat. So God fulfilled His word, "Them that honour Me I will honour."

May we all seek grace to prove to the world that the plain fare of the old Gospel and the old Book makes us truly happy and enables us patiently to endure the trials of the way.

II.

DANIEL PROSPERED BECAUSE HE STUDIED THE SCRIPTURES.

1. WHEN he left the shelter of the old home for the dangers of Babylon, he did not leave his Bible behind him. Daniel's Bible was smaller than ours but he made a good use of it. It is clear that he was familiar with the Scriptures, for he refers definitely to the law of Moses and to the prophecy of Jeremiah. He knew the history of his people and gives a little outline of it from the day in which they came out of Egypt. He heard the voice of God speaking to him and his people through the Scriptures. He was willing to be taught by the Word of God itself, and so he made his way prosperous and so had good success.

2. It was the study of the Scriptures that helped to make him the man he was. For one thing it made him a man of humble spirit. Too often promotion and pride go hand in hand. But although Daniel attained to an exalted position he still retained the spirit of humility. To mention only one illustration of

this, he said, "As for me this secret is not revealed to me for any wisdom that I have more than any living." Most of us think he was a very wise man, but he took no credit to himself, he gave God all the glory.

3. His study of the Scriptures not only made him humble and wise, but had something to do with his being a prophet himself. He learned from the prophets which were before him, but God gave him new and wonderful revelations specially concerning the rise and fall of Gentile dominion. The people of God are watching with ever-deepening interest the unfolding of events foretold by Daniel thousands of years ago. May we all learn from Daniel the importance of Bible study in the Christian life. The same way to prosperity is open to us that was open to him. "This Book of the law shall not depart out of thy mouth but thou shalt meditate therein day and night that thou mayest observe to do according to all that is written therein, for then thou shalt make thy way prosperous, and then thou shalt have good success."

III.

DANIEL PROSPERED BECAUSE HE PRAYED.

HE knew how to lay hold of divine strength and so he became strong—he had power with God and prevailed. God heard and answered the prayers of Daniel, and two of heaven's princes were sent down to help him on his knees. Unbelievers tell us that prayer accomplishes nothing, although the exercise of it may do us good. This is like telling a man that has lost his purse that he'll never find it, but searching for it may help him.

The story of Daniel contradicts these notions, for he accomplished great things by the power of prayer alone. Look at the instance recorded in chapter 2. When Nebuchadnezzar forgot his dream the wise men of Babylon were to be slain if they failed to make it known with the interpretation. That seemed a most unreasonable demand, but Daniel and his companions made it a matter of special prayer to God and the secret was revealed. "There is a God that revealeth secrets."

1. Daniel always found subjects for prayer and reasons for coming to the throne of grace. Look at his prayer as recorded in chapter 9. and we find him praying for his people. He was a true Israelite and loved his brethren. He remembered them that were in bonds as being bound with them. He pleaded for their return from captivity, which he knew was ordained of God. If we love the people of God we will show our love by praying for them. He also prayed for Jerusalem. It grieved him that the city was laid waste which was once the joy of the whole earth, and he longed to see it restored to its former glory. So should we have the welfare of the Church of God at heart, and pray continually that God would bring her back to the days of first love. He also prayed for the glory of God, and that the day might come when the whole earth should know that Jehovah was ruler in heaven and among the sons of men, and doubtless he prayed for himself that he might not be uplifted with pride nor fall into sin of any kind.

2. Daniel had special times of prayer. He was a very busy man—Prime Minister of Babylon—yet he kneeled upon his knees three times a day and prayed and gave thanks before his God. Daniel's prayerfulness would

help him through the day's business and make his trials easier to bear. Prayer would do the same for us all. It is like the policeman at a busy crossing, it compels all the rush and cares of the day to stand back.

3. Daniel had a special place of prayer. There are some who always pray best by the old arm-chair, and on the spot where they have so often unburdened their hearts before God. But for those who cannot always pray in the same place, it is good to know that

"Where'er we seek Him He is found,
And every place is hallowed ground."

You may remember the case of Nehemiah. The king asked him a question which he could not answer without divine guidance, and he says, "So I prayed to the God of heaven." He had no time to move from where he stood yet he sent up his request and God heard him.

4. Then Daniel had an attitude in prayer. He prayed with his windows opened toward Jerusalem. He could not then go over to the city he loved, but he would look that way. Possibly he had an eye to the temple and the altar, for it was a day of symbol. But that day is now passed. We have no altar but

Christ Himself, and to Him we turn our eyes when we pray. Our window is open to that Jerusalem above and towards that altar whereof they have no right to eat which serve the Tabernacle. May we all be kept in the spirit of prayer as Daniel was.

"With our windows open toward Jerusalem,
   While as captives here a little while we stay
For the coming of the King in His glory,
   Let's be watching day by day."

IV.

DANIEL PROSPERED BECAUSE HE HAD COURAGE.

1. THROUGH the whole book he appears as a man who had the courage of his convictions. He had courage to stand alone for what he knew to be right and to face the risk of being called singular and narrow-minded. He had courage to stand before Nebuchadnezzar and tell him his dream and its interpretation. He had courage to face Belshazzar too. He stood alone amidst that godless throng, and pointing to the mysterious writing on the wall he proclaimed the monarch's doom. The lion's den was a still

greater test of his endurance, but even there his courage was as firm as ever. But why should such a man as this be thrown to the lions? Well, I suppose it was because Daniel had his foes as all good men have. If ever a man was cordially hated it was Daniel, and those who hated him were no fools. They were clever, cunning, far-seeing men. They were all jealous of Daniel's promotion and so determined to put him out of the way; so they laid a plot for his destruction although they could find no fault in him because

2. His life was blameless. He had "a good report of them that are without." They tried to find something against him but were forced to confess, "We shall not find any occasion against this Daniel except we find it against him concerning the law of his God." If the same could be said of God's people to-day, what a testimony they would be in the world. Remember Daniel lived a blameless life in most unfavourable surroundings—in a court reeking with lust and cruelty. Then let no one say, "If only circumstances were more favourable, what a saint I could be." Remember Daniel and learn from him that holiness and communion with God do not depend upon surroundings but upon the will of the man himself. A gentleman was passing

through the grounds of a flower show after the show was over. Two geraniums attracted his attention. One was in a beautiful pot and had a beautiful name but it had won no prize —it looked withered and sickly. The other one had won a first prize. It was in a very plain pot, but the flower was fresh and beautiful, and it bore a label with these words, "Grown in a back-yard." So the fair flower of a blameless life may flourish in unlikely places. There were saints in Cæsar's household, and they were more saintly saints because they were there. But in spite of Daniel's integrity and prayerfulness his foes determined to destroy him.

3. They laid their heads together and drew up a flattering address and the king swallowed the flattery. Not long after it disagreed with him, and he fain would have got rid of it, but he couldn't. Things were all now shaped and ready for the destruction of Daniel. They had got their decree signed that "whosoever shall ask a petition of any god or man but of thee, O king, he shall be cast into the den of lions." That decree was passed with no intention of getting obedience to it, but only for the slaying of one faithful man of God. The plot went on the calculation that whatever happens this man may be trusted to do

what God tells him no matter who tells him not to do it—and their calculation was right. "When Daniel knew that the writing was signed, well, what did he do?" Did he say, "I wonder could I not circumvent these devils." "Can I not meet craft with craft?" No, Daniel had no notion of trying craft or cunning, he had something better. When he knew the writing was signed he went and prayed and gave thanks as he did aforetime. He made no alteration. He was found at the same place, at the same hour, and in the same spirit. But now Daniel must pay the penalty. He is thrown to the lions, but he spent a happier night in the lions den than the king did in his palace, and in the morning he was able to testify "My God hath shut the lions mouths so that they have not hurt me." So Daniel was taken up out of the den. After that everything worked out for Daniel's honour. The king approved him, admired him, loved him. Everybody in the city would hear that Daniel had been saved from the lions den, and with what awe they would look upon him. He seems to have had smooth sailing ever after. The counsellors never troubled him any more—the lions took charge of them.

V.

DANIEL PROSPERED BECAUSE HE BELIEVED.

1. HE was pre-eminently a man of faith. He had learned to trust God in youthful days, and in old age he still trusted Him. He could say with David, "O God, Thou art my trust from my youth." It was his implicit confidence in God that carried him triumphantly through all the testings of a long and eventful life. Well did he prove the truth of his own words, "The people that do know their God shall be strong and do exploits." To Daniel God was more than a mere name— He was a living bright reality. He knew Him as his own God. In this book he is distinctly called "The God of Daniel." Daniel knew Him as the God of wisdom and power. He says "Blessed be the name of God for ever and ever, for wisdom and might are His." To this God he trusted his life, his character, his reputation, his all, and God was faithful to him and never failed him once. "They who trust Him wholly find Him wholly true."

2. The den of lions was the greatest trial of his life, but when he was taken up from it

"no manner of hurt was found upon him because he had trusted in his God." That is probably the basis of the reference in Hebrews 11, "Who through faith stopped the mouths of lions," and when Paul lay in Rome, shortly before his martyrdom the experience of Daniel seemed to be in his mind as he wrote to Timothy: "I was delivered out of the mouth of the lion." But he adds, "The Lord shall deliver me from every evil work and will save me to His heavenly kingdom."

So faith may or may not bring external deliverance. True deliverance is that which brings us to our eternal home. Paul went home by martyrdom, but the martyrdom was the deliverance, a great army of saints have passed to the heavenly kingdom by martyrdom, some by the sword, some by crucifixion, some by the martyr fires, and some by the lions' den. The world and the Devil thought these were defeated, but they were only delivered. If it were possible for us to ask that noble band the question—"Was thy God whom thou trustest not able to deliver thee?" With one voice they could answer—"In all these things we are more than conquerors through Him that loved us."

Gideon.

THE Book of Judges is a record of man's failures and of God's faithfulness. Again and again they sinned and fell under the power of their foes. Again and again God heard their cries and raised them up deliverer. This section gives the story of their oppression by the Midianites. From early times they had shown themselves the enemies of God's people. It was the Midianites who first tried to get the curse of God upon them through Baalim. The Midianites were also masters in the art of plundering, and in the time of Gideon they settled down upon the land like the plague of locusts, destroying all food and sustenance. But God raised up a deliverer in the person of Gideon, the youngest son of an obscure family in a small tribe. His name stands among the heroes of faith in the eleventh chapter of Hebrews, and his conduct throughout this story proves his right to be there. His character has never been sufficiently admired. Preachers have given more attention to names less brilliant than his. He was a truly great man and deserves far better treatment than he has yet received. Despite his failings he was one of the greatest of the men of faith. A careful study of the life and work of Gideon would teach us many lessons of permanent value in the service of the Lord. Most of the incidents in his pathway to victory took place at night. We, too, are passing through the night, and like him we are surrounded by foes, but Gideon will show us how to overcome these foes and win the battle by the sword of the Lord and of Gideon.

I.

GIDEON AND THE WHEAT.

IN reading the life of Gideon we observe that God taught him chiefly by object lessons. Gideon's object lessons may teach us too. Let us think briefly of some of them. We have the object lesson of the wheat.

1. Gideon is introduced to our notice while threshing wheat in a secret place. Like all true servants of God he was trained in solitude. He learned to live the overcoming life in private before he conquered in public. That

wheat was Gideon's food, and he did not allow the Midianites to deprive him of it. This was his first step in the way of complete victory, hence the Lord addressed him as "a mighty man of valour." The wheat is for us a type of Christ. We must feed upon the bread of life, for only then shall we be strong to fight the battles of the Lord. But just as the Midianites deprived the Israelites of their food, so the world may come between us and Christ. He cannot be really enjoyed if the world is allowed to usurp His place. We must take time to search the Scriptures and so find strength to overcome the world.

2. It was while Gideon threshed the wheat that the angel of the Lord appeared to him with the soul-stirring message, "The Lord is with thee, thou mighty man of valour." These words from heaven should have lifted him above the trials of earth, but his answer shows that he was depressed by his gloomy surroundings. He said, "Oh, my Lord, if the Lord be with us, why is all this befallen us, and where be all His miracles which our fathers told us of saying, Did not the Lord bring us up from Egypt, but now the Lord has forsaken us and delivered us into the hands of the Midianites." In this statement Gideon goes back to the redemption from

Egypt, and from that standard judged the present low condition of his people. They were not what they once were, but he did not criticise their sins, he felt deep sorrow at such a state and confessed their sins as his own.

3. It was to this man that the Lord entrusted the task of delivering them from the Midianites. He said, "Go in this thy might and thou shalt save Israel from the Midianites; have not I sent thee?" These words embody the divine call to Gideon. But he had very low thoughts of himself, and pleaded poverty and weakness. But these are no arguments against the power of God. The humbler the instrument the more we see the divine power. God chooses weak things and foolish things, and base things and despised things, that no flesh should glory in His presence. God's answer to his doubts was the assurance of the divine presence set forth in the words, "Surely I will be with thee." His might lay in this assurance of the divine presence with him. The presence of God means the supply of all our needs as His servants. He never asks any of us to do more than trust in Him. Trust in Him, then go in this thy might.

II.

GIDEON AND THE ALTAR.

1. THE second object lesson in the story of Gideon is an altar. "Then Gideon built an altar there and called it "Jehovah Shalom." The name means "The Lord is peace or the Lord send peace." The word signifies not only peace but prosperity and success. This altar was not built for the purpose of offering sacrifice but for a memorial of Gideon's experience. An angel had appeared to him and given him the assurance that with him at least God was at peace, for He said, "Surely I will be with thee and thou shalt smite the Midianites as one man." But then there arose in his heart the question, "Is this really the voice of God to me or am I deluded." It was really God speaking that word home to his heart to fit him for the great work which lay ahead. How happy he must have felt as he soon realized that God was speaking to him and would be with him according to His promise. The Lord also cheered him with the word, "Fear not." We all need that word sometimes, and when it comes to us from the Lord Himself, our doubts and fears flee away like mists before the rising sun.

79

2. That altar was also a memorial of Gideon's peace with God. The Lord had said to him, "Peace be unto thee, thou shalt not die." God would not have His Gideon's disturbed in mind. If we are to trouble the enemy we must not be troubled ourselves. So the Lord still speaks to the heart of all His servants, "Peace be unto you." We might say that to each other and it might not mean much, but when God Himself says it to us then we feel the peace. When Jesus said, "Peace be still," the waves crouched at His feet and there was a great calm.

3. That altar also expressed the aim of the conflict and the hope which sustained him in the fight. Gideon was fighting for peace, and the hope that named that altar Jehovah Shalom was the hope that meant victory. This hope should animate every Christian warrior. We should be looking onward to the crowning day that's coming. We are on the winning side and victory is certain.

4. That altar was also an inspiration to Gideon for his work. As soon as his fears were banished and his heart at peace he gets to work. His first work was to cut down his father's grove which stood on the top of the hill and enclosed an altar to Baal. It was by

the Lord's command that he raised an altar
of earth and then brought his father's bullock
and slew it for a sacrifice. So if the Lord has
given us peace, let us seek to do some work
for Him. Let us pull down every idol and
present a sacrifice as Gideon did. Let us
present ourselves as living sacrifices which is
our reasonable service. Let us offer the sacrifice of praise continually and above all let
us be continually lifting up Christ who is both
sacrifice and altar.

III.

GIDEON AND THE FLEECE.

1. THE third object lesson in the story of
Gideon is the fleece. In the secret of
God's presence he desired this peculiar miracle. First the fleece was to be wet and the
ground dry, then the fleece was to be dry
and the ground wet. Was Gideon right in
asking for the sign? Yes, His petition was
not the voice of unbelief or of doubt but of
faith seeking to be confirmed. When an evil
and adulterous generation asked for a sign
no sign was given to it, but when faith asked
for one it did not ask in vain. Miracle was
an accompaniment of revelation in those early

days as pictures are of childhood. But in these days we have the Spirit of God and the Word of God made more sure than to require signs.

2. But what is the meaning of this sign? The main points seems to be that the fleece was to be different from the soil around it. This was to be to Gideon a sure token that God was at work. That was to be a proof of God's power to endow with qualities unlike the surroundings. Probably Gideon had no thought of anything beyond this. But with the Bible usage of dew before us we may find in the symbol a deeper meaning than it bore to him.

3. Dew is the symbol of divine grace—the dew of the Spirit which God only can give. It can freshen our drooping souls. It can give us joy in sorrow and keep us from being touched by surrounding evils. The wet fleece on the dry ground was not only a revelation of God's power, but may be taken as a pattern of what God's people should ever be. A prophet long after Gideon's time said, "The remnant of Jacob shall be in the midst of many people as dew from the Lord." We all need more of this freshness in our service for God. Without the dew the land would cease to be fruitful, and without the Spirit's work there can be no lasting blessing.

IV.

GIDEON AND THE WATER.

1. THE fourth object lesson in the story of Gideon is the water. He had blown the trumpet and raised the standard and there flocked to his side 32,000 men. The sight of such an army must have gladdened Gideon's heart, and he would say to himself, "Well, who would have thought it?" But God cares nothing for numbers if He cannot count hearts as well as heads. So He said, "The people are too many," and the proclamation was made, "Whosoever is fearful and trembling, let him return and depart from Mount Gilead." The result of the proclamation was that two-thirds of the army melted away. It must have required courage of a kind for them to confess being afraid, but the cowards were numerous enough to keep each other in countenance. They were like many in our own days who see the path of testimony and conflict but have not the courage to take it. They are camp-followers who can hardly tell why they are in the Church. So far as service is concerned they are no help, but rather a hindrance. But then there is a subtle desire for numbers with most of us because we seem

to think that there is power in numbers, yet
Scripture abounds with illustrations to the
contrary. Numbers have too often been the
occasion for the pride that goeth before
destruction. Let us put our dependence upon
the Lord God Almighty instead of numbering
the people. If we are really on His side we
will not mind how few are in the ranks with
us. God wants reality—quality rather than
quantity. So Gideon's army was reduced to
10,000, but it was still too big for God to
use it.

2. He said, "The people are yet too many,
bring them down to the water and I will try
them for thee there." The two ways of drinking clearly indicated a difference in Gideon's
men. Nine thousand seven hundred stooped
down to get as much as they could, and for
the time seemed to forget the fight; so they
were allowed to drink their fill and then go
home refreshed. They ought to have gone
with the first batch. There ought to have
been no second sifting needed. They were
men who wanted to make a show that they
were not full of fear when they had no real
heart for the fight, so they were sent home.
The others had fighting in their heads, not
drinking. The three hundred took just that
which would meet their present need and no

more, and the Lord said, "By the three hundred men that lapped will I save you." These three hundred men show us the true use of temporal blessings—just what is necessary and no more. "No man that warreth entangleth himself with the affairs of this life that he may please him who hath called him to be a soldier." These three hundred heroes had God with them and that was enough.

3. But why were all the fearful dismissed and sent home? Because fear is contagious as it is stated in Deut. 20. 8, "Lest his brethren's heart faint as well as his heart." There are still some faint-hearted people in the Church. To them there is always a lion in the way. They seldom have a word of good cheer for anybody. Their very presence has a depressing effect. A little more honest faith in God and the word of His grace would drive away their fear. Fear is the very opposite of faith. When fear begins faith ends. In the service of God we need to make the psalmist's resolve our own, "I will trust and not be afraid."

V.

GIDEON AND THE BARLEY CAKE.

THE fifth object lesson in the story of Gideon is the barley cake. The same night on which his little band was left alone after the ordeal by water, Gideon paid a visit to the Midianite camp. It was by God's command that he took that daring adventure. We can fancy how silently he crept down the hillside lest he should wake some sleeper. He put his ear to the hall of one tent and heard what his faith must have recognised as God's message to him. A barley cake was dreamed of as rolling down from a height and upsetting the tent, and the interpretation given was, "This is nothing else save the sword of Gideon, the son of Joash," so the enemy dreamed of disaster. It was God's own fulfilment of the promise that what they say would strengthen his hands for the attack. Then Gideon worshipped God whose voice he heard through the two Midianites.

1. In this dream of the barley cake we may see the providence of God. It was not by accident that this man should have dreamed just then and that he should have dreamed

that particular dream. God touched the brain of the sleeping Midianite, and he must dream and therein declare a truth which should bring confidence and courage to Gideon.

2. Again, it was singular that out of tents so numerous Gideon should alight upon the very one in which the two men were talking about him. There were so many chances against Gideon hearing that singular talk that we must say this is the finger of God. If the telling of this dream had been arranged by man and that Gideon should be there to hear it, there would have been a hitch somewhere. But as for God His way is perfect.

3. We may learn from the dream that God uses despised means. Barley cakes were not much valued as food in those days any more than now, so the barley cake was the emblem of a thing despised. God loves to take men whom others despise and use them for His glorious end. By using weak things He gets to Himself the glory. If He used only the great and the strong most of us would have to lie in the corner. How wondrously God has wrought by the very person we should have passed over without a thought. May we all hear afresh His cheering message, "My grace is sufficient for thee, and my strength is made perfect in weakness."

VII.

GIDEON AND THE TRUMPETS AND PITCHERS.

THE sixth object lesson in the story of Gideon is the trumpets and pitchers.

1. Gideon displayed strong faith in the stratagem by which the Midianites were thrown into panic. They were suddenly startled from sleep by the bray of the trumpets and the shout of the war cry, "The sword of the Lord and of Gideon." As they stumbled out of their tents they saw all around them the flaming torches which seemed to speak of an immense army. Little wonder that panic shook them and they trampled each other down as they raced through the darkness. Without stroke of weapon the victory was won, for the battle was the Lord's.

2. Remember those pitchers had to be broken for the light to shine out. The shining of the light in the darkness had to accompany the battle cry and the blowing of the trumpets. Allusion is made to this in 2 Cor. 4. 7, "But we have this treasure in earthen vessels that the excellency of the power may be of God

and not of us." Believers possess a wonderful treasure—the knowledge of Christ in their hearts. This light must not be hidden, it must shine forth from the earthen vessels that hold it. We have no weapon to wield but the sounding out of the word of the Lord and the light of a Christian life shining through earthen vessels. We have at our head a greater than Gideon, even our Lord Jesus Christ. Let us be strong in Him and in the power of His might, and let our rallying cry be, "Victory through the blood of the Lamb."

VII.

GIDEON AND THE EPHOD.

THE seventh object lesson in the story of Gideon is the ephod. This brings us to the closing scene of Gideon's history. From it learn that it is sometimes easier to gain a victory than to make a good use of it. Israel desired Gideon to rule over them, but he refused and said, "The Lord shall rule over you." If Israel had always remembered that God was sufficient and that He alone should have been their King, how many bitter lessons it would have saved them. Gideon would not displace Jehovah as the Ruler of Israel, but what he shrank from in one form he fell into in another. He asked that every man should give the earrings of his prey and Gideon made an ephod thereof. Here we see the very man who had led his brethren to victory over Midian now leading them into idolatry. If Gideon had refused the earrings as well as the throne it would have been well.

The God of Elijah

(2 Kings 2. 14).

WE learn from this chapter that Elijah had been taken away in a whirlwind to heaven and Elisha was to be the prophet of Israel in his stead. Thus God takes His tired workers home one by one and calls others to carry on the work. Elisha's task was a most difficult one, for he was called to follow one who was well nigh inimitable—called to follow the prophet of fire.

Little wonder that he felt his deep and urgent need of the God of Elijah. He had already asked for a double portion of his spirit. This does not mean that he wanted to be twice as great as Elijah was, but it means that he spoke in terms of the Old Testament and asked for the eldest son's portion, and Elijah said, "If thou see me when I am taken from thee, then it shall be so with Thee." How vividly this brings before us the parting scene between Christ and His disciples. This parting scene must ever be the standpoint for us. We must fix our gaze upon the ascended One. We must be firm believers in the power of our risen Lord.

If the work of God is to prosper in our hands, we must be men and women who can see the unseen God, and the things of God must be intensely real to us. We cannot live without the God of Elijah; we cannot serve without Him; we cannot overcome the difficulties of the way without Him. Here Elijah stood at the swiftly flowing Jordan. How was he to get across? He took the mantle which those waters had known before, and striking them with it cried, "Where is the Lord God of Elijah?" and the prophet passed over.

So still there is no real difficulty with God. He has the solution of all our problems, the answer to all our riddles. He can do as much for us as for those who have passed on before. We thank God for the good men and true who have entered into rest. We do not ask "Where are they?" but "Where is their God?" We do not need to say, "Oh, that we had Elijah and Elisha here again." We do not ask where is William Carey and John G. Paton and Hudson Taylor and Fred. Arnot, but where is the God in whom these men trusted? Well, "Where is He?" He is with us still. The Lord of hosts is with us, the God of Jacob is our Refuge.

I.

GOD CALLED ELIJAH.

THIS title carries our thoughts back over the record of this wonderful life. That life, so full of thrilling events, cannot be understood without God. First, God called him and kept him faithful to Himself when most of the nation had turned aside to idolatry. He called the right man at the right moment and sent him forth "When the enemy shall come in like a flood the Spirit of the Lord shall lift up a standard against him." This one man stood steadfast for God and His truth and wrought a revolution in Israel's camp. Men of his kind are needed to-day. The whole world seems to be running after vanity, and the knowledge of God is cast off. Men are needed who will be steadfast for God and His truth, not in theory only but in practice. Men who will be upright in business, men who will live for God in the workshops, men who will witness for Christ wherever they may be. The God of Elijah can keep us all steadfast as He kept him.

Elijah's power was not due to any qualities inherant in himself. He was a man of like passions with us—weak where we are weak, tempted as we are, sometimes discouraged as we are too easily. His great strength lay in his contact by faith with the God of Israel. He lets us into the secret in his first recorded utterance, "God, before whom I stand." His life was a constant vision of the presence of God. Wherever he went, whatever he did, he was always before Him. The consciousness that he was God's servant was the secret of his power. When natural strength and courage would fail him he steadied himself by this one thought, "God lives and I am His servant." As the servant of God he was constantly hearing the Word of God, and his one business in life was to trust and obey. Whether God told him to hide himself or show himself he was as ready for the one as the other. May we all seek for more of the spirit and power of Elijah.

II.

GOD ANSWERED ELIJAH'S PRAYERS.

1. HE prayed that it might not rain, and God heard him, against an idolatrous nation, and withheld the rain for the space of three years. He prayed again and the heavens gave rain in abundance. By his prayers he brought

back the spirit of a dead child. He was so much in touch with God that he seemed to get anything he desired. What were the secrets of Elijah's wonderful success in prayer? To begin with he was a righteous man, and the effectual fervent prayer of a righteous man availeth much. If we would pray like Elijah, we must be righteous as he was. But if we speak or act unrighteously either in the Church or the world our power in prayer is gone. "If I regard iniquity in my heart the Lord will not hear me." There is one prayer that we should all pray very frequently, "Search me, oh God, and know my heart, try me and know my thoughts, see if there be any wicked way in me and lead me in the way everlasting."

2. Elijah was very definite in his prayers. He just asked the Lord for what he wanted and looked for the answer. His prayers were inwrought by the Spirit and the Word of the Lord, and so were in harmony with the divine will. If we would learn from Elijah how to pray, our prayers would be short and to the point.

3. Elijah was very much in earnest when he prayed. James says "he prayed earnestly," or as in the margin, "in his prayer he prayed."

Some preach in their prayers, some do anything in them but pray. To call such effusions prayer degrades the name. We must be in earnest when we pray. Our thoughts must be fixed and our desires sincere. If we could feel more deeply the great need of both the Church and the world, we would pray more earnestly.

4. Elijah's prayers were full of expectant faith. He believed God could and would hear his petitions. So when the answer did not come at once he persevered. See how his endurance was tested when he was looking for the rain. He said to his servant, "Go up now, look toward the sea." He went up and looked and said, "There is nothing." And he said to him seven times, "Go again." At last the answer came and there was sound of abundance of rain. None of them that trust in Him shall be ashamed. When we can so lose ourselves in prayer that we can forget personal interest and seek only the glory of God the blessing will come. Let us seek to be upright in heart before God and He will help us to pray as Elijah prayed and give us answers like his, and although we may have nothing to do with giving or withholding rain, we may bring the blessing of God into many a heart.

III.

GOD FED ELIJAH.

HE sent him to hide by the brook Cherith, where he learned lessons to fit him for his calling. There he learned the value of the hidden life. Cherith was part of the preparation for Carmel. If we are to serve God successfully in public we must be much alone with Him in private. There also he learned the importance of being in the path of the divine will. God said, "I have commanded the ravens to feed thee there." There is emphasis on the word "there." That was the only place to which the ravens would bring his supplies. But as long as he was there God was pledged to provide for him. If we are where God wants us to be and doing what God wants us to do, He will meet our need somehow. Omnipotence hath servants everywhere. He has ways unknown to us of reaching the animal instinct, as well as the human will, and they obey Him. So the ravens brought Elijah bread and flesh in the morning and bread and flesh in the evening, and he drank of the brook. His simple faith in God was rewarded by the punctual arrival of his food twice a day without a hitch. His black servants never failed him all the time he was there. But Elijah's life like ours was subject to changes. So "it came to pass that the brook dried up." Well, what did Elijah think then. We do not know, but we do know that God had made other arrangements for him. Sometimes we, too, have to sit beside drying brooks. The friends we loved and trusted get fewer as the days go by. Perhaps those who formerly had fellowship with us have closed their hearts against us. Well, never mind, God wants us not to trust in His gifts but in Himself. Elijah's God still lives and Jehovah Jireh is His name.

> "Earthly friends may fail and leave us,
>   One day soothe, the next day grieve us;
> But this friend will never leave us,
>   Oh how He loves!"

When the brook dried up God sent His servant to Zarephath to be sustained by a widow woman. This woman was nearing the end of her own supplies—nothing left but a handful of meal and a little oil. Elijah's apparently selfish demand that his wants should be looked after first must have been a trial of her faith. But his cheering "fear not" kept it from failing. The continuance of her supply depended on her obedience to his request.

"There is that scattereth and yet increaseth."
Each day she made fresh calls upon her little
stock, and each day it remained the same.
The barrel was never full of meal but their
hearts were always full of peace, and that was
far better. With such tokens as these of God's
tender love and care, how could Elijah ever
forget that God had sent him and would care
for him to the end? If we think of what the
Lord has done for us in the days and years
that are past, we shall trust and not be afraid
of the future. May we all be enabled to trust
God as Elijah did.

IV.

GOD GAVE ELIJAH THE VICTORY ON CARMEL.

THE time had come for the nation to be
arrested on its downward course. So
the king, the people and the false prophets
were summoned to meet Elijah on Mount
Carmel. As soon as they were gathered together he rang out the pointed question, "How
long halt ye between two opinions?" To this
there was no reply, so Elijah proposed another
test. Each side was to offer a bullock and

await an answer by fire. It was no scheme of his own that he should put the Godhead of Jehovah to the test in this way. In his prayer he would appeal to God, "I have done all these things at Thy word, now let it be known that it is so."

Because Elijah had God at his back he could stand against a nation. God will never fail the man who trusts Him wholly. Elijah's test was accepted by both priests and people and the appeal to the god of fire was begun and long continued but without avail. At last the priests became frantic and leaped upon the altars but with all their gymnastics there was neither voice or any to answer.

Now Elijah turned scorner. He suggested a number of undignified positions for poor Baal. He said, "Cry aloud, for either he is talking, pursuing or journeying or perhaps indeed he is sleeping." Idolatry stood exposed as a vain show with no power to meet the need of the human heart. It was now Elijah's time to sacrifice, so he built an altar of twelve stones—a reminder of Israel's real unity. He laid the wood and the bullock in order on the altar and drenched all with water from the sea near by, and now prays that God will vindicate his own honour and let it be known that He is God in Israel. What a thrilling

100

moment that was as Elijah looked toward heaven for the answer by fire. He had not long to wait for the fire of God fell and consumed all and the people on their faces acknowledged that Jehovah was God. The prophets of Baal were immediately executed and Israel was delivered.

This old time story ought to be an inspiration to the people of God in these times. We are undergoing much the same ordeal as Elijah had to endure. False prophets and false doctrines abound. We have heathenism abroad, and modernism at home. We have troubles in the world and troubles in the Church. Sometimes it looks as though the forces of evil would triumph and even if they do, their victory will be short lived. Jesus shall reign triumphant over all His foes. "Ask of Me and I shall give thee the heathen for thine inheritance, and the uttermost parts of the earth for thy possession." "Thou shalt break them with a rod of iron and dash them in pieces like a potters vessel."

Then let us trust Him more, and serve Him better and He will lead us through to victory, though earth and hell should block the way.

V.

GOD RESTORES ELIJAH AFTER HIS FAILURE.

IT makes us tremble to think that such a man could fail. If Elijah can become weak and his courage gave way, who shall stand? We have seen him on Mount Carmel as the mighty prophet of God, a few days after he is down in a fit of despondency.

Up to this time he had been sustained by faith, he had never lost sight of God, now he is occupied with the danger and his courage fails. Jezebel had determined to put him to death and when he heard that, he arose and went for his life. Elijah failed in the very point at which he was strongest, and that's when most men fail. The wisest man did foolish things. The meekest man spoke unadvisedly. Abraham failed in his faith and Job in his patience. In Elijah's case the overstrain in Carmel brought re-action. The solitude of the desert increased his gloom. We are all fearfully and wonderfully made and our inner life is affected by our outward condition.

In times of stress and strain haven't we all been tempted to say, "Oh that I had wings like a dove, for then would I fly away and be at rest." So Elijah wanted to die. He sat down under the juniper tree and said, "It is enough, now, oh Lord, take away my life, for I am not better than my fathers." It was great folly for Elijah to wish to die—there was more need that he should continue to live. He said, "It is enough," but it was not enough. The Lord had more work for him to do and more blessing in store for him. If God had taken him at his word he would have died under a cloud and missed both the service and the blessing. At last the Lord took him home without dying at all. I wonder if he remembered that foolish prayer as he mounted upward to the skies. Now let us notice how God restored His failing servant. First, He let him have a good sleep. By tired nature's sweet restorer God gave His servant the rest he needed.

Next the Lord fed him. That meal was God's answer to his prayer telling him both that his life was needful and that God cared for him. This is the third time that God miraculously provided his food. The ravens, the widow and the angel were his caterers. Again the Lord gave him good news. He told him that He still had seven thousand who had not bowed the knee to Baal. Further God gave him that wonderful revelation of Him-

self on Mount Horeb. He revealed Himself
and His ways more fully to him. He let him
see that He does not always accomplish His
purpose by earthquake and fire, but sometimes
by a still, small voice.

Lastly, God took him into His work again.
He sent him to denounce Ahab, to rebuke
the idolatry of Ahaziah and appoint Elisha his
successor. And now the labourer's task is
o'er—his warfare is accomplished, and he
enters upon his rest and reward.

VI.

GOD TOOK ELIJAH HOME WHEN HIS WORK WAS DONE.

THERE is something unspeakably grand
about the manner of Elijah's home-going.
We cannot describe it. The Bible description
of it is given in a single sentence, "Elijah went
up by a whirlwind into heaven." Like the
rest of us he had many things to keep him
down—wicked Ahab and cursing Jezebel
would have put him down and kept him down
for ever. But no power earthly or Satanic
can keep a man down indefinitely if God has
destined him to rise. So Elijah went up at

last and left all his foes behind him for ever. He went up to heaven. Some present-day theologians are not sure whether there is such a place. Thank God we are not dependent upon their opinion.

"We know there's a bright and a glorious land
    Away in the heavens high,
Where all the redeemed shall with Jesus dwell,
    And you'll be there and I."

We, too, are destined to rise, "For the Lord Himself shall descend from heaven with a shout, with the voice of the Archangel, and with the trump of God: and the dead in Christ shall rise first. Then we which are alive and remain shall be caught up together with them in the clouds, to meet the Lord: and so shall we ever be with the Lord" (1 Thess. 4. 16-17).

Simon Peter.

SIMON PETER is one of the most prominent and interesting characters in the New Testament records. No name is mentioned so often in the four Gospels as Peter's name, except the name of the Lord Himself. The study of Peter's life and work would be full of interest and instruction, but for the present we must concentrate attention on the one outstanding and painful incident of his life—his fall and restoration.

The Spirit of God has recorded the story of this four times in the New Testament, so it must be of four-fold importance. This story has encouraged many wanderers to return, it has also proved to many a solemn warning. It reminds us of the frailty of the best of men. It brings tears to our eyes to think that such a man as Peter could fall. Since he fell we need to remember the warning, "If any thinketh he standeth let him take heed lest he fall" (1 Cor. 10. 12). We are all in the place of trial so long as we are in this world. As the Israelites were tempted in various ways in the wilderness, so we may expect to meet temptation of various kinds on the way. The world, the flesh and the devil are against us, and nothing can keep us safe in temptation's hour but the mighty power of God—"Kept by the power of God through faith" (1 Pet. 1. 5).

We may also learn from this story the Saviour's restoring power and love. How tenderly He dealt with His poor, fallen disciple. How fully and freely He forgave him. He is just the same Jesus. He can still have compassion on the ignorant and on them that are out of the way" (Heb. 5. 2). We may be speaking to some backsliders even now; you may be feeling down-hearted as you think of your sin in dishonouring the One who loved you and gave Himself for you. Perhaps other Christians have avoided your company and you feel it all very keenly. Well, there is One who loves you still. You may take fresh courage and come to Him. He will forgive and restore you as He did Peter and make you a blessing to others.

I.

LET us think of the nature of Peter's sin. He denied his Lord, denied Him three times, denied Him at the very time when He was suffering at the hands of His enemies.

It is worthy of note that in Luke 22. the story of Peter's sin is interwoven with the story of his Master's suffering as though it were one of the ingredients in that bitter cup. Oh how sad that Peter should add to His sorrows. His sin was terrible. He denied his best Friend —the One who loved him and called him to Himself. His sin was aggravated because he

1. Was a true disciple. His conversion is briefly recorded in John 1. 40-42. This was doubtless his first meeting with the Son of God. He was brought to Him by his brother Andrew, who so warmly commended his new-found Saviour in the words, "We have found the Messiah." In this way he brought him to Jesus. "When Jesus beheld him, He said, Thou art Simon the son of Jona: thou shalt be called Cephas, which is by interpretation a stone." By giving him a new name Jesus claimed him as His own. How intensely he loved his Lord, and how faithfully he served and followed Him we learn from the record of his life in the New Testament.

2. Again, Peter's sin was aggravated because he was not only a disciple but an apostle. Jesus had called him, with his brother Andrew, to a special place in His service. He said, "Follow Me and I will make

109

you fishers of men, and they straightway left their nets and followed Him" (Matt. 4. 19-20). In Luke 5. 1-11 we learn of the moral work that was wrought in Simon's soul when he saw the great draught of fishes miraculously given by his Master. He felt he was in the presence of God, the Creator of all things, and cried, "Depart from me, for I am a sinful man, O Lord." He learned in the school of God the lesson of his own sinfulness, and so was qualified to be a witness for Christ. Afterward we find Peter in the apostolic band. His name always heads the list of the twelve apostles. He was a true leader in the service of Christ and in the ministry of His Word. How sad to find that Satan succeeded in bringing this man down from his high and holy calling to deny his Lord and Master.

3. Peter's sin was further aggravated by the fact that he was one of the favoured three who were permitted to be in the Lord's company on very special occasions. He was present at the great transfiguration scene in the holy mount and was an eye-witness of His majesty. He was present at the raising of Jairus' daughter and saw Him as the Conqueror of death. He was present in the Garden of Gethsemane—the scene of his Lord's suffering before Calvary. Although

favoured with all these privileges he fell and denied the Lord that bought him.

II.

LET us think now of the causes which led to Peter's fall. Evidently there had been some evil influence at work which weakened his character and made him an easy prey to the wiles of the devil.

1. There was want of watchfulness. He was entirely off guard when he slept in Gethsemane. He had not profited by his Master's warning—"Satan hath desired to have you that he may sift you as wheat." How many of God's people since have failed at this very point. At the beginning of their Christian life they watched and prayed earnestly that they might not fall into temptation, but with the passing years they became less watchful and seemed to forget about the dangers of the way, with the result that, like Peter, they fell and brought dishonour upon the Lord's Name. The shores of time are strewn with the wrecks of Christian lives and testimonies. May we learn from the failures of others that we need to be kept until the last step is taken.

111

2. We read that "Peter followed afar off." He allowed the distance to increase between him and his Master; this proved to be a source of danger to him. Safety lies in keeping close to the Lord. We fear there are many true Christians to-day who follow afar off. They have left their first love. Bible study and prayer which were once their delight are now a weariness to them. They do not attend the meetings of God's people as once they did. They have no interest in the spread of the Gospel, nor in the welfare of others. They seem to live only for what this world has to give. May the Lord restore to all such the joy of His salvation.

3. Boastfulness was another cause of Peter's downfall. He was full of self-confidence and self-sufficiency. He did not realize his own weakness. "Though all should deny thee, yet will not I" was his boast; and again, "I will go with thee to prison and to death." In these avowals the spirit was indeed willing but the flesh was weak. When the testing time came his boasted strength proved insufficient. We all need to take warning from Peter's failure. We may have long years of Christian experience, much knowledge of the Scriptures, and so think ourselves strong, but unless upheld by power divine we

FOUND FAITHFUL.

are just as likely to fall as he was. "Pride goeth before destruction, and a haughty spirit before a fall" (Prov. 16. 18).

4. The fear of man also played a part in Peter's denial. He seemed to think that the Lord's cause was a lost one, and tried to save himself. His Master was a prisoner and all the other disciples scattered, so he was smitten with fear and became a coward. His cowardice now stands in striking contrast to his courage and bravery on former occasions, when in the presence of real danger he was bold as a lion. He boldly witnessed for his Lord in most trying circumstances, but now his courage has all oozed out at his finger ends, and he finds himself weak as other men. Peter, like so many others, failed in his strongest point. Our so-called "strong points" may be a source of real danger to us. Let us seek grace to realize our own weakness and be strong in the Lord and in the power of His might.

5. Rash presumption also helped to bring him down. He went in among the ungodly crowd to warm himself at the world's fire—better for him he had remained outside in the cold. He was now in a place of real danger. "A certain maid beheld him as he sat by the fire, and earnestly looked upon him, and said,

113

This man was also with Him" (v. 56). After this another accused him, and then another, until for the third time he denied as his Master had said he would, "Before the cock crow thou shalt deny Me thrice." The Lord means His people to walk in separation from the world, and so it is never safe to be in the company of the ungodly where so many others have fallen. "Blessed is the man that walketh not in the counsel of the ungodly, nor standeth in the way of sinners, nor sitteth in the seat of the scornful" (Psa. 1. 1).

III.

PETER'S RESTORATION.

AFTER all his sin Peter truly repented and was fully restored to his Lord. It might help some other backsliders if we briefly trace the steps by which he returned—the things which the Lord used in his restoration.

1. There was the crowing of the cock. The first time he does not appear to have noticed it and so denied again and again, but the third time it seems to have gone to his heart. God has many ways of reaching a guilty heart. Science, sometimes very simple things are

FOUND FAITHFUL.

used. Some of the preaching we hear is little better than the noise that bird made, but if it brings blessing let us be thankful.

2. Then there was the Lord's look. The cock-crowing by itself would not have accomplished much, but accompanied by that wonderful look it convicted Peter of his sin. That look spoke of Christ's knowledge. It seemed to say, "I knew it all; I saw it all." So He still sees and knows us in all our denials of Him by inconsistent lives. That look spoke of Christ's pain. Peter had not thought of wounding his Master, he only thought of saving himself, but the Lord must have been deeply pained by his behaviour. Again, that look spoke of Christ's love. There was no anger in it—nothing but love. That love surpassed all human love: it was divine. That look of love must have moved his heart to sorrow, and at the same time kept him from despair. Judas saw his sin in the light of an awakened conscience and went out and hanged himself. Peter saw his sin in the light of forgiving love, and he went out and wept bitterly. Judas was never anything but a painted cheat, a mere professor, but Peter was a truly born-again man.

3. Further there was the remembrance of Christ's word, "And Peter remembered the

word of the Lord, how he had said unto him, "Before the cock crow, thou shalt deny me thrice." It is well for us all to remember the words we have heard from the Lord in days that are past, words which led to our conversion, words which helped and encouraged us on the way, words received directly from the Lord Himself through our reading of the Scriptures, and words received through others in the ministry of the Word. His Word has a wonderful power. In time of depression it can cheer us. When enemies assail or friends betray we may find in it a balm for every wound.

4. Lastly, there was Christ's prayer for him. He had made intercession for Peter and it proved effectual—"But I have prayed for thee that thy faith fail not." That prayer was answered. If we look only at Peter's denial we might think that his faith did fail, but when we look at his restoration, we know that it did not fail. Peter fell but he did not remain in the mud—he rose again and pressed onward towards the celestial city. His life after his restoration proves the reality of his faith. In some things he was a better man than before his fall. By his fall he learned the lesson of self-distrust. Satan's sifting only blew the chaff away.

IV.

PETER AFTER HIS RESTORATION.

THE reality of Peter's restoration is proved by his after-life.

1. He went out from the place and company where he had fallen. It is well for us all to avoid the place of danger. "Come out from among them, and be ye separate, saith the Lord, and touch not the unclean thing: and I will receive you and will be a Father unto you, and ye shall be my sons and daughters, saith the Lord almighty" (2 Cor. 6. 17-18).

2. He wept bitterly as he thought of his sin, showing how truly penitent he was. He seems never to have forgotten his sin, and although fully restored must have felt ashamed of it. In this connection it is in-structive to notice the special message sent to him after Christ's resurrection. "But go your way, tell His disciples and Peter that He goeth before you into Galilee, there shall ye see Him, as He said unto you" (Mark 16. 7). Why was Peter's name mentioned in this message? It meant that the risen Lord would be as

FOUND FAITHFUL.

pleased to see him as the others. He had denied that he was a disciple and might have thought, "this message is not for me." But the Lord in tender love assured him that the past was blotted out—all was right between Peter and the Lord.

3. He strengthened his brethren. "When thou art converted strengthen thy brethren." He was well qualified for this work. He could tell them of the weakness of the flesh and the bitterness of sin. He could tell of the powers of his Lord's prayer and the joys of restoration. He further strengthened them by writing two books (1 Peter and 2 Peter), in which he truly feeds the flock of God. In these writings we find echoes of his fall and restoration. "Be clothed with humility, for God resisteth the proud, and giveth grace to the humble." (1 Pet. 5. 5). "Be sober, be vigilant; because your adversary the devil, as a roaring lion, walketh about, seeking whom he may devour." (1 Pet. 5. 8). "But the God of all grace, who hath called us unto His eternal glory by Christ Jesus, after that ye have suffered a while, make you perfect, stablish, strengthen, settle you." (1 Pet. 5. 10).

4. In closing, let us notice how the Lord publicly restored and reinstated Peter. We

FOUND FAITHFUL.

have the account of this in John 21. 15-19. There had been public denial and there must be public confession. "Jesus saith to Simon Peter, Simon, son of Jonas, lovest thou Me more than these?" The name "Simon, son of Jonas" takes us back to the time before he was a disciple. It was the name by which Jesus had addressed him when he first met him. The Lord now called him by his old name, as if to remind him that he had been living the life of nature rather than of grace. The Lord next questioned him as to his love —"Lovest thou Me more than these?" His reply was very humble, without mentioning the degree of his love, he said, "Yea, Lord, Thou knowest that I love Thee." He felt that Jesus could look beneath the surface of his sin and see that in spite of the denial there was a heart that was true to Him. He repeated the question a second and third time, and received the same reply. Thrice Peter had been warned, thrice he denied, and now thrice must he be asked if he really loves the Lord. He had denied Him after being warmed at the world's fire, now he must confess Him after being warmed at the Lord's fire. The Lord accepted his confession of love and re-instated him in His blessed service. He gave him a three-fold charge—"Feed My sheep," "Tend My lambs," "Feed My sheep." But

FOUND FAITHFUL.

Peter was not only to serve, he was also to suffer.

The Lord said to him, "When thou wast young, thou guidedst thyself, and walkedst whither thou wouldest: but when thou shalt be old, thou shalt stretch forth thy hands, and another shall guide thee, and carry thee whither thou wouldest not. This spake He signifying by what death he should glorify God." Peter never forgot these words (see 2 Pet. 1. 14). They predicted for him a violent death, but the Lord's command to him notwithstanding this prospect was, "Follow Me," so he was to follow his Master both in service and suffering, in life and in death, and in all he was "Found Faithful."